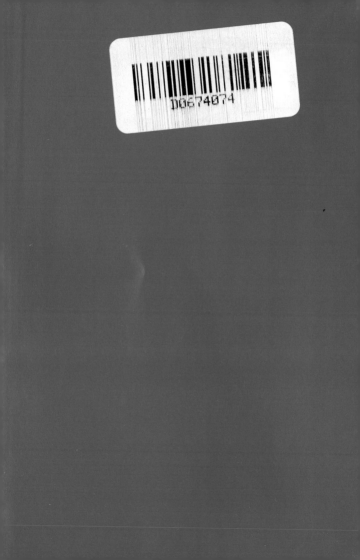

EDITED BY HELEN EXLEY

Published in 2019 by Helen Exley® LONDON in Great Britain.
Illustration by Juliette Clarke © Helen Exley Creative Ltd 2019.
All the words by Amanda Bell, Odile Dormeuil, Dalton Exley, Pam
Brown, Charlotte Gray, Helen Exley, Hannah C. Klein,
Linda Gibson, Mathilde and Sébastian Forestier, Pamela Dugdale and
Stuart & Linda Macfarlane © Helen Exley Creative Ltd 2019.
Design, selection and arrangement © Helen Exley Creative Ltd 2019.
The moral right of the author has been asserted.

ISBN 978-1-78485-203-0

12 11 10 9 8 7 6 5 4 3 2 1

OTHER BOOKS IN THE SERIES

THE LITTLE BOOK OF *Hope*
THE LITTLE BOOK OF *Gratitude*
THE LITTLE BOOK OF *Kindness*
THE LITTLE BOOK OF *Smiles*

Helen Exley® LONDON
16 Chalk Hill, Watford, Herts WD19 4BG, UK
www.helenexley.com

THE LITTLE BOOK OF

Happiness

Helen Exley

Be happy
for this moment.
This moment
is your life.

OMAR KHAYYAM

The most important thing
is to enjoy your life –
to be happy – it's all that matters.

AUDREY HEPBURN

The more you praise and celebrate your life,
the more there is in life to celebrate.

OPRAH WINFREY

Wake up with a smile –
make this the best day of your life.

STUART & LINDA MACFARLANE

Happiness may surprise you in simple moments of being there… to notice the miracle of a single morning glory open to the day.

SUSAN SQUELLATI FLORENCE

The best day is.

today! AUTHOR UNKNOWN

The sun and stars that float
in the open air... the apple-shaped Earth
and we upon it... surely the drift
of them is something grand;
I do not know what it is except that it is grand,
and that it is happiness...

WALT WHITMAN

I was set free! I dissolved in the sea,
because white sails and flying spray,
became beauty and rhythm,
became moonlight and the ship
and the high dim-starred sky!
I belonged, without past or future,
within peace and unity and a wild joy,
within something greater than my own life,
or the life of Man, to Life itself!

EUGENE O'NEILL

Little kindnesses
spread happiness.
Nothing
is ever lost.

DALTON EXLEY

I feel glad as the ponies do
when the fresh green grass starts
in the beginning of the year.

TEN BEARS,
YAMPARETHKA COMANCHE CHIEF

Gather into yourself like a bee
the hours that fall open
under the bright shaft of the sun
ripening in heat, store them
and make of them honey days.

NUALA NI DHOMHNAILL

I'm filled with joy
when the day dawns quietly
over the roof of the sky.

ESKIMO LOVE SONG

Each day
the first day:
Each day
a life.

DAG HAMMARSKJÖLD

The things that make me happy
are flowers diamonds and butterflies
and ladybirds all things that are coloured
and clowns make me laugh
and the sun and summer
and the snow makes me happy
and toys makes me and sweets
and the hedgehogs are nice
although they are prickly.

ELIZABETH WRIGHT, AGE 9

Happiness is
a warm feeling
in your tummy.

TRACEY DOWSON, AGE 8

Happiness is a lot of things.
It's snow, it's sun –
it's a thing which every day brings.
Happiness is all the world,
the beautiful things around.

EMMA SMITH, AGE 7

It is a morning in early Spring and the sun is rising, reflecting its pale shafts upon the wall. The first delicate sprays of the plum blossom lean from a jar on the table. Everywhere is very quiet, like a holy day. A blackbird, a mistle thrush and a robin are singing. Mists lie over the fields and the sky is tender blue. At rest in bed in the bare little room, pervaded by light and peace and the sweet airs of morning, there is happiness.

CLARE CAMERON

I expand
and live in
the warm day
like corn and
melons.

RALPH WALDO EMERSON

One today is worth

Happiness is a hug after loneliness.
Is sunlight after storm.
Spring after winter's ravages.
The lights of home.

CHARLOTTE GRAY

Let happiness be yours today
as you find what brings you beauty...
the fresh flowers on your table,
the fragile seashell on your desk.

SUSAN SQUELLATI FLORENCE

...wo tomorrows.

BENJAMIN FRANKLIN

There are three simple steps to happiness:

1) Smile

2) Smile

3) Smile

STUART & LINDA MACFARLANE

To have lived long enough to see
the sun, the dapple of leaves,
star-studded skies and kindly faces –
to have heard the wind, birdsong,
loving voices,
to have touched a little cat,
a woollen blanket, a flower,
to have tasted clear water, fresh bread, honey,
to have breathed the perfume
of a rose – is enough to make any life
worth the living.

PAM BROWN

The earth laughs in flowers.

RALPH WALDO EMERSON

…there is joy for me, as ever,
in not moving at all, but just basking
in the sun at the allotment,
watching the butterflies start their summer
dance, between the buddleia
and the ornamental grasses;
and reclining on my blue, stripy deckchair
in the front garden, where the foliage
of shrubs and trees – inordinately huge –
is now in full shout, curving
competitively over my head
to make a private, outdoor chamber.

BARNEY BARDSLEY

When we have
a happy heart,
we move forward.
We fly.

SRI CHINMOY

I have found such joy
in things that fill
my quiet days –
a curtain's blowing grace,
A growing plant
upon a window sill,
A rose fresh-cut
and placed within a vase,
A table cleared,
a lamp beside a chair,
And books I long have loved
beside me there.

GRACE NOLL CROWELL

I look up – and laugh

Happiness is a wonderful feeling.
It makes you feel good in any situation.
It gives you hope in times of despair.
It makes you feel peace
in a world of turmoil.

BILLY MILLS (DAKOTA)
WITH NICHOLAS SPARKS

nd love – and lift.

HOWARD ARNOLD WALTER

There are persons so radiant,
so genial, so kind, so pleasure-bearing,
that you instinctively feel,
in their presence, that they do you good,
that their coming into a room
is like bringing a lamp there.

HENRY WARD BEECHER

Sometimes days only take
a burst of sunshine,
a clump of daffodils,
a song
to flood the heart with happiness.

PAM BROWN

There is so much in the world for us all
if we only have the eyes to see it,
and the heart to love it,
and the hand to gather it to ourselves...

LUCY MAUD MONTGOMERY

Keep your face to the sunshine
and you cannot see the shadow.

HELEN KELLER
(BORN BOTH DEAF AND BLIND)

I have smelt all the aromas there are in
the fragrant kitchen they call Earth;
and what we can enjoy in this life,
I surely have enjoyed just like a lord!

HEINRICH HEINE

Life - the most wonderful fairground attraction of all - enjoy the ride.

AMANDA BELL

Today a new sun rises for me;
everything lives, everything is animated,
everything seems to speak to me
of my passion,
everything invites me to cherish it…

NINON DE L'ENCLOS

Everybody has their ups and downs
so I decided to have mine between
good and great.

DAVID HOOGTERP

My friend: It's
the song ye sing,
and the smiles ye wear,
That's a makin'
the sun shine
everywhere.

JAMES WHITCOMB RILEY

Some of the most common ideas for
spreading happiness are simple things
like smiling, saying thank you,
giving time or listening to another person
and always being positive.
Try to make these habits of a lifetime.
And imagine if you developed the one
simple habit of smiling at people –
for the rest of your life.
That would mean that you spread happiness
wherever you go. Awesome!

HELEN EXLEY

It was a lovely day of blue skies and gentle breezes. Bees buzzed, birds tootled, and squirrels bustled to and fro getting their sun-tan in the bright sunshine. In a word all nature smiled.

P. G. WODEHOUSE

May your life hav

iamond days. PAM BROWN

There is not one day of your life
that is worth wasting being sad. Be Happy!!

MATHILDE AND SÉBASTIEN FORESTIER

Write it on
your heart that
every day is the
best day
of the year.

RALPH WALDO EMERSON

The weather forecast says "Rain! Rain! Rain!"
but your heart says "Sun! Sun! Sun!"

STUART & LINDA MACFARLANE

Oh, the enchantment when,
waking from deep sleep,
we open up the house to the sounds
of the world!
How the morning air invigorates,
caressing the senses and penetrating
our whole being!
The tang of it,
the welcome it draws from us –
they take us by surprise.

IRÉNÉE GUILANE DIOH

Earth's crammed

ith heaven.

ELIZABETH BARRETT BROWNING

On a most ordinary day
something wonderful can happen.
Out of the commonplace may come
the sight of something remarkable.
Music that overturns the heart.
A sentence that illuminates the mind.
An astonishment.
A friend.
These are no ordinary days.

PAM BROWN

Close your eyes.
You might try saying…
something like this:
"The sun is shining overhead.
The sky is blue and sparkling.
Nature is calm and in control
of the world –
and I, as nature's child,
am in tune with the Universe."

DALE CARNEGIE

Life is fun

Life is happiness

Life is gladness

Life is loving

Life is helping

Life is gentleness

Life is laughter

Oh, life is beautiful.

ALLISON HUDDART, AGE 10

It's just the little homely things,
The unobtrusive, friendly things,
The "Won't-you-let-me-help-you" things...
That make the world seem bright.

Here is a gift.

A night of gentle rain.

The scent of grass.

A pattering against the window pane.

A sighing of soft air shifting

the spangled leaves.

A time to share in silence.

PAMELA DUGDALE

One must never look for happiness:

one meets it by the way…

ISABELLE EBERHARDT

Ten thousand flowers in spring,
the moon in autumn,
a cool breeze in summer,
snow in winter.
If your mind isn't clouded by
unnecessary things,
this is the best season of your life.

WU-MEN

To watch the corn grow, and the blossoms set; to draw hard breath over ploughshare or spade; to read, to think, to love, to hope, to pray, these are the things that make people happy.

JOHN RUSKIN

It's the little
sparks of
happiness
that light up
a life.

PAMELA DUGDALE

True happiness is to enjoy the present,
without anxious dependence
on the future, not to amuse ourselves
with either hopes or fears
but to rest satisfied with what we have,
which is sufficient, for those who
are so want nothing.
The greatest blessings are within us
and within our reach.

SENECA THE YOUNGER

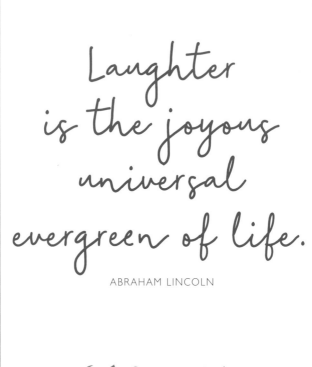

Laughter
is the joyous
universal
evergreen of life.

ABRAHAM LINCOLN

Happiness is the experience
of loving life. Being happy is being in love
with that momentary experience.
And love is looking at someone
or even something and seeing
the absolute best in him/her or it.
Love is happiness with what you see.
So love and happiness
really are the same thing...
just expressed differently.

ROBERT MCPHILLIPS

DANCE,
my heart;
O dance today
with joy!

KABIR

Winter is on my head,
but eternal spring is in my heart.

VICTOR HUGO

Happiness will allow you to feel hope
in the darkest of situations
and peace in a world of turmoil.
Happiness will allow your dreams
to come true!

BILLY MILLS (DAKOTA)
WITH NICHOLAS SPARKS

May you turn
the corner of an
uneventful day
and find wonder.

ODILE DORMEUIL

I have found joy in simple things:
A plain, clean room,
a nut-brown loaf of bread,
A cup of milk, a kettle as it sings,
The shelter of a roof above my head,
And in a leaf-laced square along the floor,
Where yellow sunlight glimmers
through a door.

GRACE NOLL CROWELL

It's a funny thing about happiness…
it just sort of sneaks up on you.
Some days I feel happy
because of the way the light strikes things.
Or for some beautifully
immature reason like finding myself
running to the kitchen
to make some toast.

JONI MITCHELL

To be happy.

To dance.

To run.

To walk for miles along the shore.

To sing like a bird.

Gather it up.

Store it like honey

to shine with a golden light,

to bring a sweetness

to your whole life.

PAMELA DUGDALE

There is beauty around us,
in things large and small, in friends,
family, the countryside,
a singing bird.
Stop to reflect, to give thanks,
to contemplate the gift
of another day.
Touch the wonders
of life and rejoice.

ANTON CHEKHOV

I hope you find joy in the great things
of life – but also in the little things.
A flower, a song, a butterfly on your hand.

ELLEN LEVINE

Each day has a rarity...
I could put it in a vase and admire it,
like the first dandelions...

MARGARET LAWRENCE

The sun shines. The rain falls.
The grass grows – the world is doing
just what it should.

STUART & LINDA MACFARLANE

The supreme happiness of life
is the conviction that we are loved.

VICTOR HUGO

Enjoy life, employ life.
It flits away and will not stay.

PROVERB

Remember this:
every time we laugh,
we take a kink out of the chain of life.

JOSH BILLINGS

Joys
are our
wings.

JEAN PAUL RICHTER

Everyday happiness means
getting up in the morning,
and you can't wait to finish your breakfast.
You can't wait to do your exercises.
You can't wait to put on your clothes.
You can't wait to get out –
and you can't wait to come home,
because the soup is hot.

GEORGE BURNS

What a lovely feeling it is
when your hope is renewed.
It's like discovering life all over again.

DALTON EXLEY

Each day
is a gift
Open it.
Celebrate.
Enjoy it.

STUART & LINDA MACFARLANE

The aim of life is to live,
and to live means to be aware,
joyously, drunkenly,
serenely, divinely aware.

HENRY MILLER

Happiness is both the beginning
and end of all the goals you have in your life.
And most important, it's the most wonderful
feeling in the world.

BILLY MILLS (DAKOTA)
WITH NICHOLAS SPARKS

My secret joy is found late at night
when a million stars are reflected
in the still surface of the lake.
I paddle out, slip down to lie on my back
in the bottom of the canoe,
and drift on the water in the silence,
held by a million points of light
above and below,
my heart breaking with the joy
of being alive on this beautiful planet.

ORIAH MOUNTAIN DREAMER

One small surprise...
A letter. A lost thing found.
Kindness from a stranger.
A skein of geese strewn across the sky.
Celandines in the ditch.
A perfect batch of scones.
A ring around the moon.

AMY POTTER

Happiness is meant for everyone
But is elusive as a butterfly.
Happiness is beautiful, as a flower.
It cannot be expressed in any rhyme.
It may only last a fraction of an hour.
But it stays inside the heart beyond all time.

E. WRIGHT

One discovers one is happy
as suddenly, as sweetly,
as if one found one's arms
filled with flowers.

ODILE DORMEUIL

So many reasons to be happy . . .
Family
Friends
Freedom
Love
Music
Sport
Laughter
You are ALIVE!

LINDA GIBSON

Happiness is found in the very littlest things.

CHARLOTTE GRAY

To fill the hour – that is happiness;
to fill the hour,
and leave no crevice for a repentance
or an approval.

RALPH WALDO EMERSON

The most complete happiness
is to work at something
you love, and to do it to the best
of your ability.

ODILE DORMEUIL

To know the reach of one's abilities,
to strive and to achieve that reach,
this is happiness.

PEARL S. BUCK

Keep a green tree in our heart
and perhaps a singing bird will come.

CHINESE PROVERB

In the woods I am blessed.
Happy is everyone in the woods.
What glory in the woodland.

LUDWIG VAN BEETHOVEN

In the depth of winter,
I finally learned that within me there lay
an invincible summer.

ALBERT CAMUS

Happiness is built
on simple foundations –
The love of beauty,
A sense of humour,
The gift of good friends.

FROM "THE FRIENDSHIP BOOK
OF FRANCIS GAY"

The only tragedy in life
is that there's so much fun
to be had that there could never be
enough time to cram it all in.

LINDA GIBSON

Keep on looking for the bright,
bright skies;
Keep on hoping that the sun will rise;
Keep on singing
when the whole world sighs...

HENRY HARRY THACKER BURLEIGH

Happiness is yours in all nature…
in fields of wildflowers and silent
deep forests, in the mystical mountains,
and the song of a distant bird.

SUSAN SQUELLATI FLORENCE

Trueᵤₑ happiness comes from the joy
of deeds well done,
the zest of creating things new.

ANTOINE DE SAINT-EXUPERY

Find expression for a joy,
and you will intensify its ecstasy.

OSCAR WILDE

Happiness is when
what you think,
what you say,
and what you do,
are in harmony.

MAHATMA GANDHI

Don't hurry, don't worry.
You're only here for a short visit.
So be sure to stop and smell the flowers.

WALTER HAGEN

Think of all the beauty that's still
left in and around you and be happy!

ANNE FRANK

Suddenly the heart lifts with joy
– finding itself part of all that is.
Sunlight and cloud,
trees, rivers,
wild geese flying.
A moment's glory.

CHARLOTTE GRAY

Paradise is

Never has the earth been so lovely
nor the sun so bright, as today...

NIKINAPI

Just remember
to fill life to the brim – and be happy.

PAMELA DUGDALE

Let happiness surprise you,
like a seashell hidden in the sand...

SUSAN SQUELLATI FLORENCE

where I am.

VOLTAIRE

Flowers always make people better, happier, and more helpful; they are sunshine, food and medicine to the soul.

LUTHER BURBANK

May you find happiness in both the central and the smallest, quietest, gentle little things.

JENNY DE VRIES

Sunshine is delicious, rain is refreshing,
wind braces us up, snow is exhilarating;
there is really no such thing as bad weather,
only different kinds of good weather.

JOHN RUSKIN

A bird. A flower.
A cloud, a gleam of sun.
A smile. A touch. A word.
Happiness comes in a thousand guises.

PAM BROWN

The happiness of life is made up of
minute fractions – the little, soon-forgotten
charities of a kiss, a smile, a kind look,
a heartfelt compliment.

SAMUEL TAYLOR COLERIDGE

Sixty seconds in every minute –
3,600 in every hour –
each one a precious diamond
to cherish and enjoy.

STUART & LINDA MACFARLANE

The best and sweetest things in life
are things you cannot buy:
the music of the birds at dawn,
the rainbow in the sky. The dazzling magic
of the stars, the miracle of light.

PATIENCE STRONG

May you not miss the happiness
in little things
while waiting for the great delights.

ODILE DORMEUIL

Sun, and sky, and breeze,
and solitary walks, and summer holidays,
and the greenness of fields…
and society, and the cheerful glass,
and candlelight, and fireside conversations
and innocent vanities and jests.

CHARLES LAMB

A happy life is not built up of
tours abroad and pleasant holidays,
but of little clumps of violets
noticed by the roadside.

DR. EDWARD A. WILSON

I am grateful for what I am and have.
My thanksgiving is perpetual.
It is surprising how contented one can be
with nothing definite –
only a sense of existence.

HENRY DAVID THOREAU

...there's the real danger of overlooking
a very important day... today.
For this is the place and the time for living.
Let us live each day abundantly
and beautifully while it is here.

ESTHER BALDWIN YORK

Sadness hears the clock stroke every hour,
Happiness forgets the day of the month.

SENECA THE YOUNGER

Stretch out your hand and take the world's
wide gift of joy and beauty.

CORINNE ROOSEVELT ROBINSON

Oh, the wild joys of living! the leaping
from rock to rock....
The strong rending of boughs from
the fir-tree, the cool silver shock
Of the plunge in the pool's living water,
the hunt of the bear,
And the sultriness showing the lion
is crouched in his lair.
And the meal, the rich dates yellowed
over the gold dust divine...

And the sleep in the dried river-channel

where bulrushes tell

That the water was wont to go

warbling so softly and well.

How good is life, the mere living!

how fit to employ

All the heart and the soul and

the senses forever in joy!

ROBERT BROWNING

Is it so small a thing to have enjoyed
the sun, to have lived light in the spring,
to have loved, to have thought, to have done?

MATTHEW ARNOLD

May your days be filled with laughter.
Spluttering laughter, whooping laughter.
The laughter that crowns success,
that springs from joy.

PAM BROWN

The first thing to be done is laughter,
because that sets the trend for the whole day.

OSHO

To make me happy I would like to make
other people happy.
I want to be nice and to help people.
I want to enjoy every minute of my life
by helping all the people
in the world when they are poorly.

LISA STANLEY, AGE 7

Earth and the great weather move me...
have carried me away...
and move my inward parts with joy.

UVAVNUK

Each and every new day
brings a new world full
of opportunities and possibilities.

STUART & LINDA MACFARLANE

Every day is

a good day.

YUN MEN

I still find each day too short for all
the thoughts I want to think, all the walks
I want to take, all the books I want to read,
and all the friends I want to see.

JOHN BURROUGHS

Look to this day! Look to this day!
For it is life, the very life of life.
In its brief course lie all the varieties
and realities of your existence:
the bliss of growth, the glory of action,
the splendour of beauty.

SANSKRIT

Happiness is the smell of the air
on summer mornings cool and crisp.

LEE WALKER, AGE 8

Whether seventy or sixteen,
there is in every being's heart
a love of wonder; the sweet amazement
at the stars and starlike things
and thoughts; the undaunted challenge
of events, the unfailing childlike appetite
for what comes next,
and the joy in the game of life.

SAMUEL ULLMAN

The importance of a happy life
can't be exaggerated.
Think of each and every day as priceless.
If you take a series of those days
and combine them, it becomes a year.
Add the years together,
and it becomes a lifetime –
a lifetime of love,
happiness, honor, hopes, and dreams.

BILLY MILLS (DAKOTA)
WITH NICHOLAS SPARKS

*Do anything,
but let it
produce joy.*

WALT WHITMAN

Happiness is the sun in the sky,
galloping on the beach,
water splashing, feeling free.

MEGHAN SIMMONS, AGE 11

If I were to choose the sights, the sounds,
the fragrances I most would want...
on a final day on earth,
I think I would choose these: the clear,
ethereal song of a white-throated sparrow
singing at dawn; the smell of pine trees
in the heat of noon; the lonely calling
of Canada geese; the sight of a dragon-fly
glinting in the sunshine...

EDWIN WAY TEALE

That it will never come again is what makes life so sweet.

EMILY DICKINSON